GEO

6/05

P9-EEN-132

WAR MACHINES

WEAPONS CARRIER HELICOPTERS

The UH-60 Black Hawks

by Michael and Gladys Green

Capstone
press

Mankato, Minnesota

Edge Books are published by Capstone Press,
151 Good Counsel Drive, P.O. Box 669, Mankato, Minnesota 56002.
www.capstonepress.com

Library of Congress Cataloging-in-Publication Data
Green, Michael, 1952–
    Weapons carrier helicopters: the UH-60 Black Hawks / by Michael and
    Gladys Green.
    p. cm.—(Edge books. War machines)
    Includes bibliographical references and index.
    ISBN 0-7368-3780-9 (hardcover)
    1. Black Hawk (Military transport helicopter)—Juvenile literature.
I. Green, Gladys, 1954– II. Title. III. Series: Edge Books, war machines.
UG1232.T72G74 2005
623.74'6047—dc22   2004012158

Summary: Describes the UH-60 Black Hawk helicopter, including its history,
equipment, weapons, tactics, and future use.

Editorial Credits
Angie Kaelberer, editor; Jason Knudson, set designer; Patrick D. Dentinger, book designer;
    Ted Williams, illustrator; Jo Miller, photo researcher; Scott Thoms, photo editor

Photo Credits
Check Six 2004/Greg Davis, 6
Corbis/George Hall, cover; John H. Clark, 14
Getty Images Inc./AFP/Marwan Naamani, 13
Sikorsky Aircraft Corporation, 28, 29
Ted Carlson/Fotodynamics, 5, 9, 11, 12, 16–17, 18–19, 21, 23, 25, 27

**Capstone Press thanks Captain Bradley Osterman, U.S. Army, for his assistance
with this book.**

1 2 3 4 5 6 10 09 08 07 06 05

Table of Contents

CHAPTER 1

The Black Hawk in Action

U.S. Army Special Forces soldiers are on a mission deep behind enemy lines. They wait for a helicopter to take them back to home base. The U.S. soldiers don't know that enemy soldiers have set a trap for them. The enemy soldiers have machine guns and antiaircraft missiles.

The enemy soldiers open fire as the U.S. helicopter comes in for a landing. The enemy soldiers think they are shooting at a lightly armed UH-60 Black Hawk transport helicopter. They quickly find out that their target is the most heavily armed version of the Black Hawk. This helicopter is the MH-60L Direct Action Penetrator (DAP).

The MH-60L DAP protects other Army helicopters.

LEARN ABOUT:

Missions

History

Black Hawk models

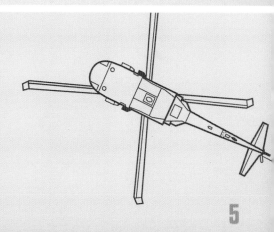

5

The UH-60A was the Army's first Black Hawk helicopter.

The helicopter's crew members fire machine guns at the enemy soldiers. The helicopter then lands and picks up the Special Forces soldiers.

As the DAP rises above the trees, an enemy missile streaks in its direction. The missile misses the DAP. A device on top of the helicopter confuses the missile's aim.

The DAP pilots spot an enemy antiaircraft vehicle in the distance. They fire a laser-guided missile at it. The enemy vehicle explodes in a ball of fire. The pilots turn the helicopter toward home base.

Helicopter History

During the Vietnam War (1954–1975), the Army used thousands of transport helicopters to move soldiers. The most useful transport helicopter was the UH-1 Iroquois. Soldiers nicknamed this helicopter the "Huey."

The Army began to look for a replacement for the Huey in the early 1970s. In 1976, the Army chose Sikorsky Aircraft Corporation to build its new helicopter. The Army began using the UH-60A Black Hawk in 1979.

New and Improved

In 1989, the UH-60L Black Hawk replaced the UH-60A. The UH-60L's engines produced more power than those of the UH-60A. Sikorsky still makes the UH-60L.

The Army's Special Forces began using the UH-60A Black Hawk in the early 1980s. Special Forces units perform dangerous, secret missions. The Special Forces Black Hawks were called MH-60As. When Special Forces started using the UH-60L Black Hawk, they called it the MH-60L. The newest Special Forces Black Hawk was first used in 1995. It is called the MH-60K.

The U.S. Air Force, Navy, and Coast Guard also use Black Hawks. Air Force pilots fly the HH-60G Pave Hawk and MH-60G Pave Hawk. The Navy calls their version of the Black Hawk the SH-60 Seahawk. The Coast Guard uses HH-60J Jayhawks.

Coast Guard members use Jayhawks during missions.

CHAPTER 2

Inside the Black Hawk

Helicopters depend on lift to fly. The air is thinner at higher altitudes and on hot days. Thin air can keep a helicopter from getting the lift it needs. The Black Hawk's two engines power the helicopter to high altitudes on the hottest days.

The two engines also make flying safer. If one engine breaks down, the helicopter can use the other engine until it can land.

Black Hawks can travel 347 miles (558 kilometers) on one tank of fuel. With two extra fuel tanks, the helicopter can travel at least 1,000 miles (1,600 kilometers).

Some Black Hawk models don't need to land to refuel. They have an in-flight refueling probe. The probe allows the Black Hawks to refuel from a KC-130 tanker aircraft. The KC-130s are like flying gas stations.

Some Black Hawks refuel on the ground.

LEARN ABOUT:

Engines

Crew members

Flare and chaff systems

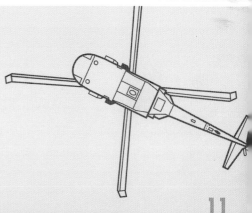

Flight Crew

The Black Hawk flight crew includes two pilots, a crew chief, and a gunner. The pilot and copilot sit side by side in the cockpit. The crew chief and gunner ride in the cabin behind the cockpit. The crew chief and the gunner fire the two machine guns. The crew chief is also in charge of any passengers or cargo in the cabin.

The Black Hawk has two pilots.

Crew members wear helmets with a built-in intercom system.

A Black Hawk cabin is about the same size as a small bedroom. It holds 11 soldiers, plus their weapons and gear. The crew members wear helmets with a built-in intercom system. The intercom system lets the crew members talk to each other during flight.

The cockpit has features that protect the Black Hawk's crew.

Protection

All Black Hawks have features that protect them from weapons. Armored cockpit seats and wing panels give extra protection to the pilot and copilot. Bulletproof fuel tanks help prevent fuel fires during crashes.

The Black Hawk also has a system that protects it against heat-seeking missiles. A heat-seeking missile has a sensor in its nose. The sensor guides the missile to the exhaust heat released by the helicopter's engine. When the missile gets close to a Black Hawk, the crew releases hot, bright objects called flares. The missile chases the flares instead of the helicopter.

Another system protects the Black Hawk from radar-guided missiles. When a missile is near the Black Hawk, the crew releases chaff. These small metal strips reflect radar waves. The enemy missile can't find its target through the cloud of metal strips.

Flying Conditions

Because helicopters fly slower than jets, they are easier targets for enemy weapons. Black Hawk pilots fly close to the ground. They use trees, hills, and buildings as cover. This action cuts down their chances of being hit by enemy fire.

Black Hawks fly close to the ground.

To fly at night, most Black Hawk pilots wear night vision goggles on their helmets. Night vision goggles help soldiers see in the dark. The goggles magnify the light of the moon, stars, or distant city lights. The crew chief and gunner also wear night vision goggles to fire the helicopter's machine guns.

UH-60L Black Hawk

Function:	Troop/cargo transport
Manufacturer:	Sikorsky Aircraft Corporation
Date First Deployed:	1989
Length:	64 feet, 10 inches (19.76 meters)
Height:	16 feet, 10 inches (5.13 meters)
Rotor Diameter:	53 feet, 8 inches (16.36 meters)
Maximum Takeoff Weight:	22,000 pounds (9,979 kilograms)
Top Cruising Speed:	184 miles (296 kilometers) per hour
Maximum Altitude:	19,150 feet (5,837 meters)
Range:	347 miles (558 kilometers)
Crew Members:	Three or four
Weapons:	Two M60 machine guns

1 **Tail rotor**

2 **Rotor blade**

3 **Main rotor head**

4 **Cabin**

5 **Machine gun**

6 **Cockpit**

2

3

UNITED STATE

4

6

5

CHAPTER 3

Weapons and Tactics

All Black Hawks carry weapons. The first UH-60A Black Hawks had two machine guns. As the Army improved the Black Hawk, it added faster, better weapons.

Machine Guns

The UH-60A's two M60 7.62 mm machine guns are on either side of the cabin. The M60 can fire 450 to 600 rounds per minute. It can hit targets about 2 miles (3.2 kilometers) away from the helicopter.

The gunner and crew chief fire the machine guns.

LEARN ABOUT:

Guns

Missiles

Rockets

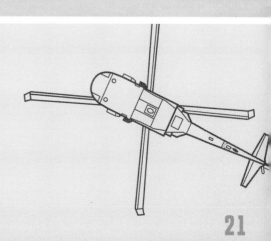

The MH-60 Black Hawk carries other machine guns. Some Black Hawks hold two M134 7.62 mm miniguns. Others carry two GAU-19 .50-caliber guns.

The M134 has six barrels connected to an electric motor. The barrels rotate at a high speed. As they rotate, each barrel fires a bullet, one after the other. The M134 can fire either 2,000 or 4,000 rounds per minute.

The GAU-19 .50-caliber machine gun has three barrels connected to an electric motor. The barrels on the GAU-19 also rotate at a high speed and fire each bullet in order. The GAU-19 can fire 2,000 rounds per minute.

The 12.7 mm bullets from the GAU-19 are much larger than the 7.62 mm bullets from the M134. The larger bullets can destroy unarmored vehicles or lightly armored vehicles.

The MH-60K carries two
M134 machine guns.

DAP Weapons

Special Forces Black Hawks perform many jobs. They destroy enemy ground targets. They gather information about enemies. They also act as armed escorts for transport helicopters. Because of these jobs, the MH-60L DAP carries more weapons than other Black Hawk models. These weapons include automatic cannons, guided missiles, and rockets.

When the DAP goes on a mission, it carries the M230 30 mm automatic cannon. The M230 can fire up to 625 rounds per minute. The ammunition can punch holes through the armor of most tanks.

The DAP also carries Hellfire and Stinger guided missiles. The Hellfire destroys tanks and other enemy targets on the ground. The Stinger is an air-to-air guided missile. It protects the DAPs from enemy planes and helicopters. The range of both missiles is about 5 miles (8 kilometers).

The MH-60L DAP carries laser-guided antitank missiles. To fire these missiles, the DAP uses a laser range finder and laser designator. Both devices shoot invisible laser beams at a target. The laser range finder measures the distance to the target. The laser designator bounces laser light off a target to guide the missiles to the target.

The DAP also carries rockets. It can carry 70 mm unguided rockets called Folding-Fin Aerial Rockets (FFAR). The newest FFARs have a range of about 5 miles (8 kilometers).

The DAP carries 70 mm rockets.

CHAPTER 4

The Future

The Army plans to rebuild about 1,200 of its existing Black Hawks. The rebuilt model will be called the UH-60M.

Sikorsky plans to update 60 Black Hawks and produce 10 new UH-60Ms each year. The Army should get its first UH-60Ms in 2006.

Structural Upgrades

The UH-60M has improved engines. These engines increase the helicopter's speed by about 20 miles (32 kilometers) per hour. They also allow the UH-60M to carry about 2,000 pounds (900 kilograms) more weight.

The UH-60M has stronger rotor blades. These blades will need fewer repairs than the current blades do. The new blades also help the helicopter fly better in hot weather and at high altitudes.

The Army plans to upgrade most of its Black Hawks.

LEARN ABOUT:

Updates

UH-60M

Electronics

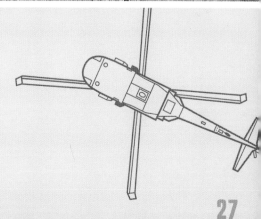

Interior Upgrades

Better electronic systems are part of the UH-60M. The cockpits have color displays instead of the dials that are on current Black Hawks. The UH-60M also has new radios and a digital map system. The system shows the helicopter's location on a computer monitor.

The UH-60M's cockpit has color displays.

Each UH-60M has a monitor that shows the location of friendly and enemy forces. The information can come from space satellites, other helicopters, or even soldiers on the ground. Pilots will use this information to avoid enemy weapons and find friendly soldiers.

Army leaders plan to use the Black Hawk until at least 2025. The UH-60M will bring many more years of Black Hawk service to the United States and the world.

Glossary

altitude (AL-ti-tood)—the height of an object above the ground

ammunition (am-yuh-NISH-uhn)—bullets and other objects fired from weapons

armor (AR-mur)—a heavy metal layer that protects against bullets or bombs

chaff (CHAF)—strips of metal foil dropped by an aircraft to confuse enemy radar

laser beam (LAY-zur BEEM)—a narrow, intense beam of light

missile (MISS-uhl)—an explosive weapon that can fly long distances

radar (RAY-dar)—equipment that uses radio waves to find and guide objects

rotor (ROH-tur)—machinery that spins a set of rotating blades; rotors allow helicopter pilots to lift or steer an aircraft.

upgrade (UHP-grayd)—to improve something

Read More

Budd, E. S. *Military Helicopters*. Military Machines at Work. Chanhassen, Minn.: Child's World, 2002.

Holden, Henry M. *Black Hawk Helicopter*. Aircraft. Berkeley Heights, N.J.: Enslow, 2001.

Tomajczyk, Stephen F. *Black Hawk*. Enthusiast Color. St. Paul, Minn.: MBI, 2003.

Internet Sites

FactHound offers a safe, fun way to find Internet sites related to this book. All of the sites on FactHound have been researched by our staff.

Here's how:

1. Visit *www.facthound.com*
2. Type in this special code **0736837809** for age-appropriate sites. Or enter a search word related to this book for a more general search.
3. Click on the **Fetch It** button.

FactHound will fetch the best sites for you!

Index